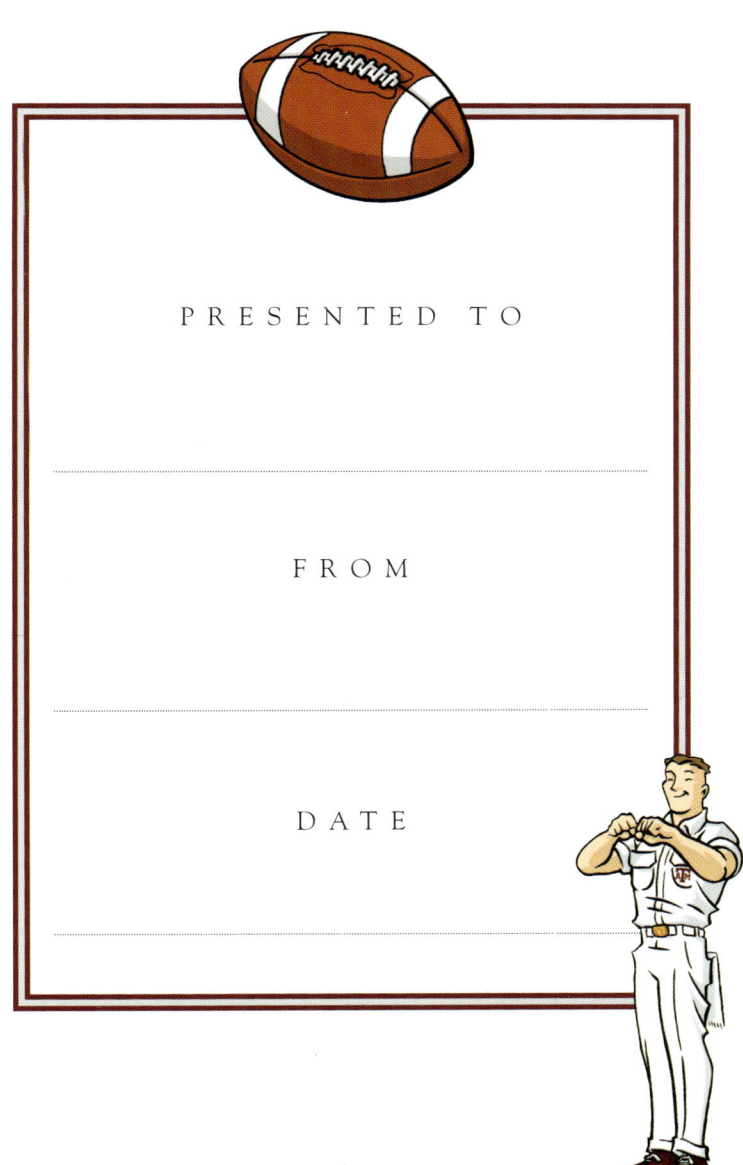

Special Thanks: Travis Raine & Danielle Reedy, two great Aggies!

Edited by Jerre Borland

Text copyright ©2007, Jady Regard
Illustrations copyright©2007, Pete Moriarty
All Rights Reserved.

No part of this book may be reproduced or copied in any form
without the written permission from the publisher.

All trademarks are the property of Slice of Lime Publishing
New Iberia, Louisiana
www.sliceoflime.net

ISBN: 978-0-9789475-1-4

10 9 8 7 6 5 4 3 2

First Printing, July 2007

Printed in United States
through Walsworth Publishing Company
and Four Colour Imports, Ltd.,
Louisville, Ky.

Book Designed by Glen Clark
www.fieldspan.com

To Dr. Bill Nash
For introducing me to all things Aggie!

Howdy! Today is the day I have been waiting for my whole life. Today is the day my Dad takes me to my very first Fightin' Texas Aggie football game. We are heading to College Station, the home of one rough, tough football team. I can't even begin to tell you how excited I am about our trip.

Once we arrive on the Texas A&M campus, I grab my football so Dad and I can spend some time throwing passes to one another. We also work on some runs up the middle, a couple of sweeps, a few options and a handful of toss-outs. Dad says we have to keep the other team guessing!

After loosening up, we find a great place to tailgate. All of the old Ags share good bull about football teams of the past. Stories of the Wrecking Crew kept me on the edge of my seat. Most importantly, everyone was marooned out! I don't think I have ever seen so much maroon in one place before.

Out of the corner of my eye I catch a glimpse of the Fightin' Texas Aggie Band as they make their way to the stadium. Senior boots and silver spurs sparkle in the sun as each member of the band moves in perfect formation. There isn't a cadet out of place.

Just behind the band, Reveille, the first lady of Aggieland, makes her grand appearance. Surrounding her are the cadets of Company E-2, they care for her day and night and make sure she never misses a big event like a home football game.

Dad says no trip to an Aggie football game would be complete without a visit to the 12th Man statue. The 12th Man represents all of the students and fans that fill up the stadium each Saturday during football season. It's a tradition in Kyle Field for the 12th Man to stand ready during the entire game, showing their support for the team.

Finally we arrive at Kyle Field. The Stadium is huge and so tall! A long walk to our seats provided us with the chance to practice our favorite yells. Dad and I went to Yell Practice the night before, so we knew every word. "Farmers fight! Farmers fight! Fight! Fight! Farmers, farmers fight!"

Kyle Field is home to the 12th Man and nobody leads the 12th Man like the Yell Leaders. The Yell Leaders are also called the Keepers of the Spirit. Running to their spots along the sidelines in their white, pressed uniforms, the Yell Leaders instruct the 12th Man to yell on cue for their Aggies.

Standing on our feet we watch as the ball is kicked high into the air. The game has begun! The real 12th Man races down the field with his teammates, looking to make a big tackle. A giant clash of helmets is followed by a pile up of maroon jerseys.

Forming at the north end of Kyle Field is the Fightin' Texas Aggie Band. They always march to an undefeated halftime performance and I do not want to miss one note. When the visiting band hits the field my Dad and I split to get a hotdog and my first Kyle Field souvenir, my very own 12th Man towel!

The score of the game is tied until nearly the end, when suddenly the Aggie quarterback drops back and throws a bomb. The Aggies score! The 12th Man cheers; the cannons fire and the band plays. A touchdown puts the Aggies on top for good.

After watching the big victory during my first visit to Kyle Field, it is now time to saw Varsity's horns off! We sway back and forth to the Aggie War Hymn. Cadets rush the field and carry the Yell Leaders away to the fish pond.

Hullabaloo, Caneck! Caneck!
Hullabaloo, Caneck! Caneck!

All hail to dear old Texas A&M,
Rally around Maroon and White,
Good luck to the dear old Texas Aggies,
They are the boys who show the fight.
That good old Aggie spirit thrills us.
And makes us yell and yell and yell;
So let's fight for dear old Texas A&M,
We're goin' to beat you all to –
Chig-gar-roo-gar-rem!
Chig-gar-roo-gar-rem!
Rough! Tough!
Real stuff! Texas A&M!

Good-bye to Texas University.
So long to the Orange and White.
Good luck to the dear old Texas Aggies,
They are the boys who show
the real old fight.
The eyes of Texas are upon you,
That is the song they sing so well,
So, good-bye to Texas University,
We're goin' to beat you all to –
Chig-gar-roo-gar-rem!
Chig-gar-roo-gar-rem!
Rough! Tough!
Real stuff! Texas A&M!

Saw Varsity's Horns Off!
Saw Varsity's Horns Off!
Saw Varsity's Horns Off!
Short!

Varsity's Horns are Sawed Off!
Varsity's Horns are Sawed Off!
Varsity's Horns are Sawed Off!
Short!

Back at home my Dad comes into my bedroom to tuck me in for the night. "Dad," I say, "I can't tell you enough how much fun I had at the Aggie football game and how nice it was to spend the whole day with you. I loved Kyle Field. I can't wait to go back again. And I think you are right, I was **born to be an Aggie**!"

My Favorite Aggie Autographs